201

GREAT QUESTIONS

FOR PARENTS & CHILDREN

JER

NavPress ◢
BRINGING TRUTH TO LIFE
P.O. Box 35001, Colorado Springs, Colorado 80935

The Navigators is an international Christian organization. Our mission is to reach, disciple, and equip people to know Christ and to make Him known through successive generations. We envision multitudes of diverse people in the United States and every other nation who have a passionate love for Christ, live a lifestyle of sharing Christ's love, and multiply spiritual laborers among those without Christ.

NavPress is the publishing ministry of The Navigators. NavPress publications help believers learn biblical truth and apply what they learn to their lives and ministries. Our mission is to stimulate spiritual formation among our readers.

The people quoted in this book each have profound and thoughtful words worthy of our consideration. However, using their quotes for the purposes of this book in no way implies that we necessarily endorse or agree with all of their beliefs or values.

ISBN 1-57683-147-7

Printed in the United States of America

1 2 3 4 5 6 7 8 9 10 11 12 13 14 15 / 05 04 03 02 01 00 09

FOR A FREE CATALOG OF
NAVPRESS BOOKS & BIBLE STUDIES,
CALL 1-800-366-7788 (USA)
OR 1-416-499-4615 (CANADA)

Contents

INTRODUCTION

The Power of the Question

In the midst of juggling schedules, guiding our children, helping them with school projects, participating in church activities, and keeping food on the table, we far too often miss the joy of discovering things together as a family.

Our children especially love to be listened to, to be known. That is one of the primary ways they experience our love and their self-worth. As author and theologian Sam Keen says, "Nothing shapes our lives so much as the questions we ask." If we are going to continue learning about one another and deepening our sense of family, it is necessary to continue asking questions—and listening.

That's what this book is designed for, to help you more deeply connect with those in your life that you hold most dear. This is not a book of answers. Rather, it is a toolbox full of ready-to-use questions to help renew that discovery experience. Not only will it allow parents to gain more insight into the ticking parts deep inside their children, but it also will allow children to learn more about their parents, their joys and pleasures, their values, faith, hopes, and dreams—the lessons of life learned along the way. And beyond the fun and bonding that can occur, it can provide the children assurance that their own struggles, fears, questions, and disappointments are natural, normal feelings and experiences.

Use this little book to help you celebrate each

other, to listen, to learn, to remind you of why you are family, of what holds you together, of what makes each of you unique. To give your family relationships new shape and meaning. And to help you to not (in the words of John Michael Talbot) be "preoccupied with the superficial at the expense of the meaningful."

A Few Suggested Goals and Guidelines

1. The goal is to stimulate healthy, two-way conversation between parents and children (the sort of thing that you might not take or find the time to do on your own). Use this book

- in conversations around the dinner table
- while traveling in the car (keep a copy in your glove box)
- before or during family devotions
- during Saturday morning breakfast
- at bedtime

2. Questions are intended to be answered by parents too. (For example, when a question asks about a parent or grandparent, the parents need to talk about *their* parents or grandparents.) In fact, it would be helpful if the parents occasionally go first in answering the question to help serve as a model for honesty, openness, playfulness (where appropriate), and willingness to talk about the subject. The more honest and

authentic parents can be when answering, the better they will model trusting responses from the children. (Note to parents: In some ways, many of these questions may be harder for you to answer than for your children, as they often have fewer protective layers. The better you can go below the surface with your answers—in appropriate ways, of course—the better the children will follow your lead and respect you for your authenticity and honesty.)

3. Some questions are intended to be serious, some more playful and humorous. But all are intended to help you discover a little more about each of the special gifts who make up your family. Remember that in most cases these are not intended to be questions requiring right or wrong answers. The purpose is not to argue about an answer or get a good grade but to learn about the feelings, thoughts, and values of each other—to develop trusting, intimate bonds. Use this as a tool to help improve or enhance your conversations and mutual discovery times together.

4. Keep in mind that often just one question, along with other thoughts or feelings it may bring to mind, can require quality time. That's okay. It is better to go slow and gain deeper understanding—plus have fun in the process—than to race through this book. View this small, handy resource as a longtime companion that you go back to again and again. (One way to use this book is to each take turns choosing a question to begin a family discussion.)

5. Questions are not designed to be a way to pry into difficult areas where a family member may be uncomfortable to go. Nor is the information revealed during these sharing times meant to be used against

someone later. Treat this sharing and discovery process as confidential and sacred.

6. Questions are intended for all family members, ages five and up. You will note that the book begins with easier, less vulnerable questions and progresses to deeper, more thoughtful topics. Go at your own pace. But feel free to break the rules if so inclined. This is one book you are not required to read from front to back. You have permission to rephrase the questions in any way that might better suit your family.

7. And finally, remember that God models for us an intense desire to know us and to listen to every expression of our hearts. Invite Him to be with you in this family-building growth and discovery process.

How to Use
This Book in Groups

While the questions in this book are designed to be used within a family, they can easily be adapted for use in a group of children or of children and parents. For example, a Sunday school teacher or kids' club leader might want to use one or two of these questions as openers at the beginning of their session each week. If you want to use the questions in a group, all you have to do is rephrase a few of them. In most cases it's just a matter of changing pronouns around.

INSTEAD OF:
How would you describe each member of **our** family to someone who has never met **us** if you had no photos to help you?

ASK:
How would you describe each member of **your** family to someone who has never met **them** if you had no photos to help you?

There's plenty of room on each page to pencil in your rewording ahead of time, if you wish.

Whether this book is used by kids and parents in their family times or is used in groups, my prayer is that it may begin many warm, invigorating conversations in families.

WARM-UP

QUESTIONS

1

What story do you most enjoy hearing your parents or other relatives tell about something you did or said when you were little?

2

Make believe your hands are tied
behind your back. How will you
open the refrigerator to get
a snack?
How will you brush your teeth?
What will be the hardest
thing for you to do?

3

If you were an airplane pilot,
would you rather fly high
or fly fast? Why?

4

How could the three blind mice
run after the farmer's wife —
since they could not see?

5

What was the best reward you ever received for a job well done or for good behavior?

6

Who is crazy about you, and how
does that person show it?
Who was crazy about you when
you were a young child?

7

What do you do when someone
you care about is angry with you?
How does it make you feel?
Is it always your fault when
someone is angry with you?

8

In what ways are people
most like dogs?
If the members of our family
were dogs, what kind of dog
would each person be? Why?

9

What are five things
you love to do?
What are five things
you hate to do?
What would happen if you
never had to do the things
you hate to do?

10

Do you think having lots of
money is important?
Why or why not?
What would you do if you
had lots of money?
What would you do if you
had no money?

11

What are five things
on your wish list?

12

What do you worry
about most and why?

13

What is one thing you would love to smash with a hammer if you would not get in trouble for doing so? Why?

14

If you were lost in a forest, how would you find your way home?

15

Why did God make aardvarks?

16

If our house caught on fire,
how would you escape?

17

What invention can you imagine that would allow us to eat spaghetti without making a mess? What is your favorite messy food?

18

When someone you don't know very well invites you to do something together, how can you tell if it would be a good thing to do?

19

If you were given a magic seed,
what do you hope it
would grow into?

20

What do you get most tired
of waiting for?

21

If you had never smiled before in your life, what is it that might finally make you smile?

22

What is the most out-of-
the-ordinary pet you can think of?
Would you like to have such a pet?
Why or why not?

23

What is a true story you
remember about a mouse
or a snake?

24

What five words would you
use to describe Jesus?
What do you like most
about Jesus?

25

When are you most
frightened of the dark?
What helps you not be afraid?

26

Where is your favorite
place to explore?

27

Tell about a time when you told
one of your friends about Jesus.
If you've never told anyone about
Him, why do you think that is?

28

Of all those in our family,
who do you most like
to hear pray? Why?

29

If, as a family, we were going to do something kind for someone else, what would you like us to do? For whom?

30

Tell about a recent time when you got goose bumps.

31

Do you believe you have a personal angel? Why or why not? If yes, do you think your angel is living in our home?

32

If you were to run away from home, where would you go? When do you most feel like running away? Why?

33

Who makes you feel most welcomed when you get home? How does he or she do this?

34

If we were to have a family
talent show—
and everyone in the family
had to participate—
what would you do in the show?
What would you enjoy
seeing other members
of our family do?

35

If you were a very, very
small animal, what would you
like to be?
What if you were a very, very
large animal?
Which would you most
like to be? Why?

36

When do you most like
to be hugged?
When are you most likely to be
embarrassed by a hug? Why?

37

If we as a family were to
do whatever you wanted us to
do one day each month,
what are some of the things you
would want us to do?

38

What is it you love to
smell the most?
What is it you love to
taste the most?

39

When you see a stranger crying,
are you more likely to think
the person is crying from joy
or from sadness? Why?
What is the best way to tell why
someone is crying?

40

Are you more like an empty
bottle being filled or like a
candle being lit? Explain.

41

Make believe you are a spy.
If your identity becomes known,
you will be thrown into jail.
How will you disguise yourself to
keep your identity a secret?

42

If people had to be trained how to live in a house like pets do, in what area would you still need more training? Why?

43

Do people know you mostly
as someone who talks or as
someone who listens?
What is the hardest part
about doing the opposite?

44

What are three things you like
or appreciate about your dad?
Your mom?
Each sister or brother?

45

If you opened an ice-cream store and it was going to have totally new, never-tried-before flavors, what would be three of your flavors?

46

Pretend that our family is going to get a new baby. What are your fears and your wishes about this new arrival in our home?

47

What makes Sunday a special
day in our home?

48

Who are three of your favorite
relatives (cousin, uncle,
grandmother, and so on)?
Why have they become
special in your life?

49

If our family lived two
hundred years in the
future instead of today,
what do you think
would be different?
How would your
bathroom be different?
Your bedroom?
Your vehicle?
Your food?
Your toothbrush?
Your hairstyle?

50

What are some other ways
God might have designed
the human body?
For example, what is
another way
He could have created
us to move?
Where else could
He have designed
our eyes to be?

51

Why are people usually so quiet in an elevator? What is the funniest thing you've ever done (or can imagine doing) in a crowded elevator?

52

What is one of your favorite
worship songs that you like
to sing to Jesus?
What do you like about it?
Why do we sing worship songs?

53

Imagine for a moment that your life is a voyage to a distant land. Will you be traveling mostly by land or by sea? Why? What are the things that will cause you the greatest delays or problems on this voyage? What kinds of dragons or sea monsters will you have to slay along the way?

54

Which of your close friends
most inspires you to be a
better person?
How does he or she do this?
How do you inspire your friends
to be better people?

55

If you could spend a year living with another family in a different country, what country would you choose? Why? What would be most interesting and enjoyable about such an experience for you? What would be the hardest?

56

What does the word *respect*
mean to you?
How does one gain respect?
When is it that you feel most
respected and admired?

57

If you could visit any factory to see how something is made, what factory would it be?
What is something you'd like to learn during such a visit?

58

When were you most
tempted to quit?
What did you learn
from this experience?

59

Who would you be if you
could be someone famous?
Why this person?

60

What was the name of one of
your great-grandfathers or
great-grandmothers?
Where was this person born and
what did he or she do?
What would you most like to
know about this person?

61

When was a time
you felt rejected?
What happened to make
you feel that way?
What changed, if anything, as a
result of the experience?

62

Who most reminds you of Jesus?
Why? In what ways do you wish
you were more like Jesus?

63

If you could give just one gift —
any gift at all,
regardless of the cost —
to the person of your choice,
what would this gift be and
who would you give it to?
If someone else were to give you
any gift, what would you want
him or her to give you?

64

When you hear a rumor, what
is the best way to determine
if it is true or false?
Has anyone ever started a rumor
about you? If so, tell about it.
Have you ever started a rumor
about someone else that you later
were sorry for?

65

Other than a relative, who
is the one person you feel
closest to? Why?
Could you tell this person
your deepest secrets?

66

What are three of your top
God-given talents and abilities?
What are you doing to develop
these talents?

67

Describe a time when you were blamed for something you did not do. How did it make you feel? How did you react?

68

How would you describe each member of our family to someone who has never met us if you had no photos to help you?

<u>69</u>

What three things cause you to
feel stressed out at home?
At school or work?
How do you usually act when
you feel this way?
What do you do to get
unstressed?

70

If you were to create another Mount Rushmore, what four people would you choose to depict on the mountainside? Why?

71

What is it you think you deserve
in life right now? Why?

72

Who is the biggest
tightwad in our family?
In what ways?
What are the possible good things
about being tight with money?
Bad things?

73

If you were to make it a rule
that you would do at least
one nice thing
for yourself every week,
what are at least five things you
would do for yourself?
Are you doing enough nice
things for yourself now?
Why or why not?

74

What are five silly things you've
never done but think would
be fun to try?

75

If you went away on a one month trip, in what ways would you be missed by our family? What are your responsibilities that someone else would have to pick up? In what ways would you be irreplaceable?

76

What are three dreams you have
for your life that you currently
think are impossible?

77

What's an example from your
life when saying no to
something meant saying
yes to something else?
Are there ever any
exceptions to this "rule"?
If yes, when?

78

Tell about a time when you lost something you cherished — and then found it.
Tell about a time when the item was never found.

79

What is the scariest thing you can imagine yourself doing? Why is this so scary to you? What would it take to work up the nerve to do this?

80

Think for a moment about one
of your favorite Bible stories
(David and Goliath, Daniel in
the lions' den, or whatever).
Why is this one of your favorites?
What is something you learn
from this story that helps
you today?

81

For you, what has been the most fun vacation or outing our family has ever taken? Why? If you could pick the next family vacation, what would it be?

82

What was a change
you had to make that was
difficult for you (new school, new
city, new house, and so on)?
Why? What did you learn from
making this change?

83

Imagine that for an entire
year our family has been
planning a week-long trip to
Disney World (or some other
fun getaway spot). Two weeks
before we are to leave, you are
given an opportunity to earn five
thousand dollars in one week
doing something you enjoy—
but it is the same week you
are scheduled to be gone
for the family trip.
What will you do: take the job or
go on the trip? Why?

84

In what ways is our house
like your body?
What do they both require?
What is something
your body needs that our
house does not need?

85

What is it that determines when
a child becomes an adult?

86

What is one of the first things
you notice about someone
who has a good attitude?
What is one of the first things
you notice about someone
with a bad attitude?
Who has the most influence
in determining your attitude—
others or yourself?

87

If there were no limitations, what is something great you would like to accomplish in your lifetime? Why?

88

What are five qualities that make a good friend? Do you have these qualities? If not, how can you develop them?

89

If you were a sleepwalker, what would be one of the most embarrassing things you might do?

90

What is one of the most
important things your mother
or father ever taught you?
How have you put that
lesson into practice?

91

Imagine for a moment that you
are like a baby bird in a nest.
In what area of your life do you
most need to be
"pushed out of the nest"
so you can learn how to "fly"?

92

If you had traveled with the
wise men to visit baby Jesus,
what special gift would you
have given Him? Why?

93

How do you know when
God speaks to you?
What is the hardest part for you
about listening to God?

94

If our family decided to give only handmade gifts next Christmas, what are three different things you might make as gifts? What would you enjoy about this kind of Christmas? What would you not enjoy?

95

Which of your senses—
hearing, seeing, touching,
tasting, or smelling—
would you miss most if
you lost it? Why?
In what ways might your life
actually be better if you were
deprived of this sense?

96

Other than members of
our immediate family, who
is your hero?
What is it about this person
that makes him or her a hero
in your eyes?

97

Imagine that someone has just given you an expensive gift—but it is something you already have. Will you tell the giver that you already have the item, or will you say thanks and pretend it is something you will cherish? Why?

98

What is your favorite story about something mischievous your parents did as children or teens? How does this story help you better understand your parents?

99

In what ways are you generous?
In what ways do you wish you
were more generous?
Tell about someone who was very
generous with you.

100

When was a time you got in big trouble for something you did? What did you learn from that experience?

101

What is the most difficult thing about being a kid? What is the most difficult thing about being a parent?

102

If our family were to have an awards ceremony, who in our family would be most deserving of the following awards?

- loses the most things
- best physical condition
- best dish washer
- good neighbor award
- best sleeper
- worst driver
- best comedian
- neatest
- life of the party
- most like a cartoon character

103

When are you most likely to believe someone is paying attention to you?
How does this make you feel?
When are you least likely to believe you are being paid attention to?

104

What is the most nutty or goofy
thing about our family?
In what ways is this a good
or a bad thing?

105

Pretend that someone has given
you enough money to design and
build a home for our family.
The home can be built anyplace
you want and can be as big or
small as you want it to be.
Describe this house and
where it is.

106

What are two of your happiest
childhood memories?
What is one of your most
embarrassing childhood
memories?

107

Who has the hardest time saying,
"I love you," in our family?
Who has the easiest
time saying that?
When is it hardest for you to
say those words?

108

If we had a monthly night of family crafts, what would you enjoy doing for our next craft night?
What is your favorite thing you've ever made? Why?

109

When you first meet someone, are you more likely to trust or mistrust that person? Why?
What does it mean to trust someone?

110

If you had the power to be invisible any time you wanted to be, how would you use this power? Would this power be helpful or unhelpful? In what ways?

111

Would you rather be rich or famous? Why? Is it possible to be one without the other? Explain.

112

To you, does our family feel
most like a hotel, a church,
or a foreign country? Why?

113

Where do you feel
most frightened?
Where do you feel
most safe? Why?

114

Think for a minute about the first house or city you can remember living in as a child. What are the things you most liked (or like) about it? If you could have chosen any other place to grow up, where would it have been?

115

Would you rather have plenty of money or plenty of good, trustworthy friends? Why?

116

FOR PARENT: What are three things you did as a child that your children do not have to do or do not get to do— and that you wish they did?

FOR CHILD: What are three things your parents did as children that you do not do— and that you wish you did? Why?

117

What kinds of things
hurt your feelings?
Has anyone ever hurt your
feelings without realizing it?

118

If God hired you to design
heaven, what would it be like?

119

If you were required to have a secret code to indicate you are a member of the family before you could enter the house, what would your secret code be?

120

If our family were to write
a book of humor,
what would be some of the
funny things people in our family
have said or done that you would
want to include in this book?

121

Billy Graham once said,
"I want to be remembered
as someone who was fun
to live with."
What makes a person
"fun to live with"?
What do you most want to
be remembered for?

122

If for Christmas you were
given the gift of time—
one hour every day for a year
that you could spend with any
friend or family member—
what are five things you'd love to
do with this extra hour?

123

In some cultures, people are given a new name when they reach a certain age or milestone in life.
If you were given a new name, what would you like it to be?
Why?

124

In what ways do you feel
celebrated in our family
just for who you are?
In what ways do you feel
celebrated for your
accomplishments?

125

What is a personal
accomplishment someone
in our family other than you has
achieved that makes you proud?

126

In what three ways have you
found kindness to be
contagious in our family?

127

In what ways do you feel
your privacy is respected
in our family?
In what ways do you wish you
had more privacy?

128

What attitude or quality
of someone in our family
do you admire?

129

Where do you most feel
green and alive in your life?
Where do you most feel
tired or discouraged? Why?

130

If our family decided to leave
the TV off for a full month,
what would be the hardest
part about this for you?
What would you like about it?
How would you spend
your extra time?

131

What is it you'd most like
to ask God?

132

What do you think might
make God laugh?
What might make God cry?

133

Why do you think God
wanted you to be born?
When is God most pleased
with you?

134

If you were to stop doing
something that you frequently do,
what would you stop doing? Why?
What would the rest of our family
think if you stopped doing this?

135

Are you more likely to be
unhappy because of things that
don't happen to you or because of
things that *do*? Explain.

136

If a national TV program
or magazine announced
that you were the best there ever
was at something you like to do;
how would it change your life?

137

Is love stronger than hate?
Why or why not?
How have you seen this
to be true?

138

How would you answer
the following?

In our world, _____
        could never happen.

In our city, _____
        could never happen.

In our family, _____
        could never happen.

I, personally, would never, ever

_____.

139

What is something that probably won't happen, but that would really be fantastic if it did? How would this "something" change your life if it happened?

140

In what ways is something old better than something new? What is an example of this? Name something old you own that you would not want to exchange for something like it that is new.

141

If you had the power to rewrite all of the world's rules, what would five of your new rules be? In what ways would these rules help people live together peacefully?

142

What have you done in the past month that has helped you build your self-confidence? Where do you need more confidence?

143

If you were trying to please
Jesus—and no one else—what
would you do differently today?
In the past month?

144

Would you rather be a
substitute on a winning team
or a star player on a losing team?
Why?

145

What does it mean
to have courage?
Who is the most
courageous person you know?
When was a time you did
something that required courage?

146

Who has something you
wish you had?
Why do you want this thing?
How would having this thing
make you a better person?

147

If you had the power to
read other people's minds,
how would you use this power?
Whose mind would you
most like to read?
In what ways is it a good
thing that we cannot read
other people's minds?

148

What do you need more of
in your life right now?
What can you do to
make this happen?

149

If our family decided to spend one week each year helping others, what would you like our volunteer service to be this year?

150

What is the area in your life where you are seeing the most improvement lately?

151

If aliens from another planet were
to live in our home for a month,
what do you think they would
find most unusual
about our family?
What would they most enjoy
about being in our home?

152

What would you do differently
if you had the chance to do
it over again?

153

If our family were to do something totally different (such as become farmers, ranchers, missionaries, tour guides, restaurant owners, lighthouse keepers, or circus entertainers), what would you most like us to do? What would you miss about your current life if our family did this?

154

What is something you have a
really hard time believing?

155

Tell about the loss of a friend
(such as from moving away,
a disagreement, or death)
that has been hurtful for you.
What do you most miss
about this friend?

156

Do rich people have more
friends than the rest of us?
Why or why not?

157

If you were to do something
athletic that you've never done
before, what would it be?

158

When have your fears turned out
to be exaggerated or unnecessary?
If you were completely fearless,
what is something you
would like to do?

159

Most families have several
rules of the house, such as
"Don't talk with your mouth full."
What are five of our
family's rules?
What are the consequences when
these rules are disobeyed?
Which of these rules would you
like to change? Why?

160

What was the meanest trick
anyone ever played on you?
How did it make you feel?

161

In 1997 the computer
"Deep Blue" beat the world
chess champion in a chess match.
Do you think computers will
someday be able to "think" as
well as humans—or even better?
Why or why not?

162

What is it you most remember
your parents telling you about
what they thought or felt when
they first laid eyes on you?
What is it you would most like to
know (or be reminded of) about
the day you were born?

163

In what ways do you think the
world is getting better?
In what ways is it getting worse?
If you could make any three
changes in the world,
what would they be?

164

Who in our family is most
different from you?
Who is most like you?
In what ways are you able to be
yourself with both people?

165

What sort of compliment
means the most to you?
What do you usually say or do
when receiving a compliment?

166

Who is the best storyteller
in our family?
Why do you enjoy listening to
this person tell stories?
What are some favorite stories
you enjoy hearing from
this person?

167

Which Bible character,
other than Jesus, would you most
like to talk with?

168

If Jesus suddenly appeared to
you in person today,
what would you want
to ask Him?

PROBE

QUESTIONS

169

Would you rather have
experiences or things?
What makes you
choose this way?

170

What is something you have from
your grandparents that serves as
a good reminder of the qualities
and characteristics you want to
remember about them?
What would you like to
pass along to your
grandchildren someday?

171

In what ways do you live your life in the shadows? In what ways do you live your life in the light?

172

Healthy change often requires that we give up something we enjoy. What is a change you'd like to see in your life — and what is something enjoyable you'd be willing to give up for this change to occur?

173

If it were possible to pour dreams
into a cup like you pour juice,
would your cup be mostly
full or mostly empty?
What dreams would be
in your cup?

174

What makes you feel loved?

175

What do you do that you
don't want anyone but our
family to know about?
What is one thing you'd like all
our friends to know about?

176

Do you believe that God picks in advance a specific time and way for us to die? Why or why not?

177

Is everything that happens to us meant to be?

178

In the story
"Beauty and the Beast,"
the Beast is kind and good on the
inside but ugly on the outside.
In what ways does your outside
keep people from knowing who
you really are on the inside?
What do you wish people
knew better about who
you are on the inside?

179

What tends to make you
suspicious? Give an example.

180

If we could reverse roles
for a week—
parents becoming children and
children becoming parents—
what would you do that you
cannot do now?
What would be the hardest
part about this change?

181

What is one thing you would like to invent or discover in your lifetime?
In what helpful ways might this invention change the world?

182

If you could start your own company, what would it do or make?
What would you most enjoy about running your own company?

183

When do you feel most misunderstood?
What do you do when you feel misunderstood?

184

If you knew you did not have to be perfect at it, what new skill would you like to try out?

185

When did you first realize your parents were not perfect?

186

Imagine you are skydiving and your parachute fails to open. On the way down you have three minutes to think about everything you will not get to do. What are five things that you will most regret not being able to do before you die?

187

What does it mean to
honor your parents?
What is one way you honor
your mom and dad?

188

Imagine that seven hundred years from now archeologists will be exploring the ruins of our home. What do you think they will find most fascinating in your bedroom?

189

Pretend that you are a judge.
Two people are standing before
you, each swearing that he
is telling the truth,
but they are contradicting
each other.
What would you do
to determine which one
is telling the truth?
Can you tell if people
are telling the truth just
by looking at them?

190

If you were to take a pilgrimage to someplace that has a strong connection to our family's historical past, where would you go? Why? What is it you'd like to learn about our family history on this pilgrimage?

191

Imagine for a moment that the order of our lives has been reversed—we are born as old people and grow younger until we die as helpless babies. What do you like or not like about this? How will getting a job, getting married, or having children be different? What would be the purpose of your life?

192

What part of your personality are you most likely to hide from others for fear of being disliked?

193

Is there a right or wrong choice for every decision you make in life? Explain.

194

What is the difference between doing things right and doing the right things? What is an example of each?

195

What would make you a more likable person?

196

If our family were going to
make a movie together,
what would you like the
movie to be about?
What role would you prefer
to have: producer,
director, camera operator,
actor, scriptwriter,
set designer, make-up artist,
or wardrobe assistant? Why?

197

What is the hardest part about being totally honest with a friend? Would you tell the truth if you knew for certain that you would lose friends or popularity?

198

If it were totally up to you, what would you set as the three primary goals for our family? Why?

199

If you were to write a book about your life, what would the title be?

200

What is something in your life
that is both bitter and sweet?
In what ways?
What do you notice most:
the bitter or the sweet?

201

If you knew for certain that there
was a safety net to catch you,
where would you most like to
take a leap in your life?

Author

JERRY JONES is a free-lance writer working on his first historical novel. Over the past twenty years he has helped edit, write, or develop more than twenty-five books, served as editor of three national periodicals, and helped launch a national ministry. He values time with both his immediate and extended family and loves serving as the editor of a biannual family newsletter. Jerry lives in a creekside cottage in the mountains near Colorado Springs, Colorado.

IMPROVE YOUR SMALL GROUP
AND PERSONAL RELATIONSHIPS.

201 Great Questions

Ideal for getting conversations started in small groups or for
hanging out with friends, this book gives you the opportunity
to learn more about others--and about yourself.

201 Great Questions
(Jerry D. Jones) $6

201 Great Questions to Help Simplify Your Life

Evaluate those difficult-to-balance tasks and obligations to
bring into focus the things that really matter. Re-direct your life
into simpler patterns that affect your thinking and daily habits.
Useful for both individual and group reflections.

201 Great Questions to Help Simplify Your Life
(Jerry D. Jones) $6

201 Great Questions for Married Couples

Here's an in-depth resource to get beyond the surface to the
topics that really matter. Whether you've been married five or
fifty years, this creative communication tool will enhance your
relationship. Useful for both individual and group reflections.

201 Great Questions for Married Couples
(Jerry D. Jones) $6

Get your copies today at your local bookstore, visit our website
at www.navpress.com, or call (800) 366-7788 and ask for offer
#2296 or a FREE catalog of NavPress products

NAVPRESS
BRINGING TRUTH TO LIFE
www.navpress.com
Prices subject to change.